High-Impact Presentations

Robert W. Pike, CSP

Provant Media Publishing
4601 121ST Street
Urbandale IA, 50323-2311
1-888-776-8268
www.provantmedia.com

High Impact Presentations

Robert W. Pike, CSP
Copyright © 1995 by Robert W. Pike, CSP

This publication is designed to provide accurate and authoritative information in regard to the subject matter covered. It is sold with the understanding that neither the author nor the publisher is engaged in rendering legal, accounting, or other professional service. If legal advice or other expert assistance is required, the services of a competent professional should be sought.

Credits:
Provant Media Publishing:

Managing Editor:
Editor:
Designer:
Cover Design and Illustration:

Art Bauer
Todd McDonald
Leigh Lewis
Karen Massetti Miller
Dave Kirchner
Gayle O'Brien
Kevin Zdenek

Published by Provant Media
4601 121ST Street
Urbandale IA, 50323-2311 and
Resources for Organizations, Inc.
7620 W. 78th Street
Edina, MN 55439

Library of Congress Catalog Card Number 97-75605
Pike, Robert W.
High-Impact Presentations

Printed in the United States of America
1997
ISBN 1-884926-35-5

Introduction

When asked what we fear most, many of us would put public speaking high on our lists. In fact, numerous surveys indicate that the only thing that seems to surpass it is the fear of dying. Almost every presentation seminar is chock full of people from all walks of life who want to learn how to present with confidence in front of a group. If speaking to a group is so fearful, why do we want to learn how to do it?

Some of us don't have a choice because of the nature of our vocations, or, perhaps, avocations. Since we have to make presentations, we want to learn how to do it in the best possible way. Others of us simply present as a part of our personalities. We are naturally verbal and like to talk. We will speak in front of anybody—even very small groups of two or three. Then, there are those of us who want to make a difference. We have a passion for an idea, a cause, or a problem to be solved. We want to enlist others to help us implement the idea, solve the problem, or further the cause. We know the more skillfully we present our case, the better the results will be.

Why present with excellence and impact? Because, rightly or wrongly, we are judged by the way we present. A high-impact presentation can enhance our reputation, help us enlist others to get the job done, and open the doors to opportunities that might otherwise remain closed. Powerful presentations can be important tools to succeeding in business and in life.

The purpose of this book is to give you practical tips, tactics, and strategies that can enhance the impact of your presentations whether to groups of 1 or 1,000. There are several ways you can view this book. If you view it as a novel, it makes a lot of sense to read it from beginning to end. Or, you can use it as a cookbook, picking and choosing ideas. In the same way you don't have to try every recipe in a cookbook to make a great meal, you don't have to try every idea in this book to give a great presentation. Above all, consider it a resource, something that you can refer to time and time again. The ideas contained in this book can enhance any presentation you want to give.

About the Author

Robert W. Pike has developed and implemented training programs for business, industry, government, and the professions since 1969. Beginning as a representative for Master Education Industries, he received nine promotions, in three and one-half years, to Senior Vice President. His responsibilities included developing an intensive three-week Master Training Academy covering all phases of sales training, management development, communications, motivation/platform skills, and business operations. During his five years as Vice President of Personal Dynamics, Inc., that company grew from less than 4,000 enrollments per year to more than 80,000. He pioneered undergraduate and graduate credit on a national basis.

As president of Resources for Organizations, Inc. and Creative Training Techniques International, Inc., Bob leads sessions over 150 days per year covering topics of leadership, attitudes, motivation, communication, decision making, problem solving, personal and organizational effectiveness, conflict management, team building, and managerial productivity. More than 60,000 trainers have attended the Creative Training Techniques workshop. As a consultant, Bob has worked with such organizations as Pfizer, Upjohn, Caesars Boardwalk Regency, *Exhibitor* Magazine, Hallmark Cards Inc., and IBM. A member of the American Society for Training and Development (ASTD) since 1972, Bob has been active in many capacities, including three National Conference Design Committees, Director of Special Interest Groups, and a member of the National Board of Directors.

Since 1980 he has been listed in the Who's Who in the Midwest and in the current edition of Who's Who in Finance and Industry. Over the years Bob has contributed to magazines like *Training, The Personnel Administrator,* and *The Self-Development Journal.* He is editor of the *Creative Training Techniques* newsletter. He is author of *The Creative Training Techniques Handbook, Development, Marketing and Promoting Successful Seminars and Workshops,* and *Improving Managerial Productivity.*

The Creative Training Techniques Companies

The Creative Training Techniques Companies (CTT) trains trainers! We assist clients in achieving exceptional training results with the application of innovative and creative training and development technologies.

CTT's train-the-trainer seminars combine high-impact material with participant-centered techniques to give you practical, useful tips and tactics. Learn how to involve your participants, capture and keep their attention, teach and review in less time—all with the Creative Training Techniques process!

CTT conducts four different train-the-trainer public seminars in over 200 nationwide locations. These seminars build trainers' competencies with instructor-led, participant-centered techniques, tactics, and tips.

We also offer fun, stimulating, creative resource products to enhance trainer's programs and personal abilities. Whether it's *Tricks for Trainers, Powerful Presentation Music, Making Training Stick,* or handpointers, CTT-endorsed products will impact your programs and help you produce better results.

For seminar brochures, in-house information, or a product catalog call (800)-383-9210 or (612) 829-1954, or fax us at (612) 829-0260.

60,000 trainers can't be wrong!

● Table of Contents

Chapter One

Why Create High-Impact Presentations?　　　8

Why Present?　　　8
Conquering Your Fear of Presenting　　　11
Self-Check: Chapter 1 Review　　　13

Chapter Two

Types of Presentations　　　14

Six Presentation Formats　　　14
Outline Formats　　　17
　Providing Information　　　17
　Teaching a Skill　　　20
　Reporting Progress　　　23
　Selling a Product, Service, or Strategy　　　26
　Obtaining a Decision　　　29
　Solving a Problem　　　32
Self-Check: Chapter 2 Review　　　35

Chapter Three

Organizing and Preparing Your Presentation　　　36

MindMapping　　　36
Organizing a Presentation　　　41
Putting It All Together　　　45
Self-Check: Chapter 3 Review　　　46

Chapter Four

Opening and Closing Your Presentation　　　48

Opening a Presentation Effectively　　　48
Types of Openings　　　49
Closing a Presentation Effectively　　　56
Types of Closings　　　57
Self-Check: Chapter 4 Review　　　61

Chapter Five

Asking and Answering Questions 62

Asking Questions to Involve Your Audience	62
Tips on Asking Questions	63
Answering Questions to Reinforce Your Message	67
Two Common Q & A Mistakes	67
Tips for Answering Questions	69
Pitfalls When Answering Questions	71
Self-Check: Chapter 5 Review	73

Chapter Six

Using Handouts in Your Presentation 74

Why Handouts Are Important	74
When to Hand Out a Handout	78
What to Put in a Handout	78
Handouts Can Make the Difference!	82
Self-Check: Chapter 6 Review	83

Chapter Seven

Presentation Problems and Solutions 84

Problem 1: My Presentation Is Boring	84
Problem 2: I Have Too Many Vocal Pauses	86
Problem 3: I Get Nervous Before and During a Presentation	87
That's All There Is to It	89

Answers to Chapter Reviews 90

Chapter *One*

Why Create High-Impact Presentations?

Chapter Objectives

▶ Understand why presentations are important.

▶ List the reasons you might be called on to give a presentation.

▶ Describe how a presentation impacts your professional credibility.

▶ Know why people fear presentations.

Why Present?

No matter what your profession, you will probably give a presentation in the next 12 months.

No matter what your profession or job—manager, salesperson, doctor, quality team member, etc.—you will probably give a presentation of some kind in the next 12 months. How you do it will either raise or lower your credibility and make a difference in your ability to influence others. Here are some of the most common reasons you may give a presentation.

♦ **It is expected.**
Whether because of the position you hold, the work you have done on a project, or the information you possess, you are the one expected to make the presentation. Managers are expected to give oral reports on the accomplishments of their departments. Supervisors are expected to update employees on company policies. Salespeople are expected to deliver group presentations on their products or services to potential customers. Controllers are expected to present quarterly results. Quality team leaders are expected to report on the status of the work their teams are doing.

Whether we like it or not, all of these situations (and many more in the workplace) require live oral presentations.

◆ **It is a way to stand out.**
We live in a competitive world. An effective presentation allows you, as well as your knowledge, talent, and abilities, to stand out from the rest of the crowd.

◆ **You have no other choice.**
You'd rather do anything but present, but the information can't be put in written form or can't be delivered by someone else, and it must be made known. Like it or not, the best person to make the presentation is you.

◆ **It is the best way to communicate.**
Information can be delivered in a variety of formats. It can be passed along in a memo, presented in a formal written report, scripted, narrated, and put on audiocassette. Sometimes, however, the best method is a live presentation that allows for interaction as well as questions and answers. A live presentation ensures communication of both the sum and substance of the material. It also provides a forum for clearing up any misunderstandings.

> **A live presentation ensures communication of both the sum and substance of the material.**

◆ **You have passion for the subject.**
This is probably the best reason for giving a presentation. You may not always be able to express your passion completely in a memo or report. A presentation gives you an excellent way to convey your enthusiasm.

Take a Moment

Identify the many presentations that are delivered at your workplace. The following are some examples for thought starters. Add to the list. Make the list as complete as possible. List all presentations no matter whether they are delivered by you or someone else.

- Group sales presentations
- Budget presentations
- Departmental status reports
- Quality presentations
- Customer service presentations
- Team meeting presentations
- Training presentations
- Vendor presentations
- Customer/client presentations

_____

_____

Look over this list, select the presentations that are most familiar, and answer this question: What kinds of problems are caused when these presentations are not delivered effectively?

_____

_____

Now think about some poor business presentations you've seen. (They probably weren't delivered by you!) Why were the presentations so ineffective?

_____

_____

Finally, what are some of the consequences of poorly delivered business presentations?

_____

_____

Conquering Your Fear of Presenting

Many people pass up opportunities to make presentations, and this negatively impacts their careers. They usually avoid presentations because of one of these fears:

1

◆ Fear of making a mistake

◆ Fear of forgetting

◆ Fear of looking foolish

Believe it or not, you can eliminate 75 percent of all nervousness and fear from your presentations. To do this, you must enter the presentation knowing in your heart that you are prepared. You must know your material and how you will present it. You must have support materials (handouts and visual aids) that are properly prepared. Finally, you must practice your presentation. The more effort you put into preparation and practice, the more confident you will be when you present.

The more effort you put into preparation and practice, the more confident you will be when you present.

As you continue through this book, remember the Six Ps—they are what high-impact presentations are all about:

Proper Preparation and Practice Prevent Poor Performance

To be prepared you must:

1. Analyze your presentation content.

2. Know your audience.

3. Select an outline format and develop an outline.

4. Develop support materials, such as handouts and visual aids.

5. Research presentation details, including the room setup, the availability of audiovisual equipment, and the format of the meeting (especially the agenda items immediately before and after your presentation).

As you read this book, you will learn the best ways to perform many of these preparation steps.

Self-Check: Chapter 1 Review

Indicate True or False for each of the statements below.
Suggested answers are given on page 90.

_____1. A business presentation provides you with the opportunity to showcase your knowledge, talent, and ability.

_____2. Fear of failure is one reason people avoid business presentations.

_____3. Good presenters are born with the ability to present.

_____4. Developing the ability to give a good business presentation can accelerate your career.

_____5. Proper preparation and practice can help eliminate the fear of forgetting.

_____6. Support materials, such as handouts and visual aids, are not necessary for most business presentations.

_____7. Preparing for your presentation includes checking the room setup for the presentation and checking the availability of audiovisual materials.

Chapter *Two*

Types of Presentations

Chapter Objectives

▶   Understand six types of presentations.

▶   Choose an appropriate format for your presentations.

Six Presentation Formats

The type of presentation you give depends on its purpose. In business, there are six types of presentations commonly used. Let's examine each of them. Keep in mind, however, that not every presentation that you will want to make will lend itself to one of these formulas, but they are a good place to start. Then, you can modify, adjust, and adapt to meet your specific needs.

Type 1: Providing Information

■   Your organization is considering going to five different trade shows. Your presentation might provide information on the five different trade shows, the demographics of the attendees, and their purchasing power. Or, the presentation might be on the final day of the conference and the purpose of your presentation would be to inform people of next year's time, date, and location, as well as what they can expect to see and hear.

Type 2: Teaching a Skill

■   You have installed a new security system, and you are making a presentation to the staff on how to disarm the security system when entering the premises, how to notify the monitoring company when on the premises, and how to rearm the system when leaving the premises.

Type 3: Reporting Progress

■ Your company has launched an "In-Touch" calling campaign. Each person in the company is calling current and past clients to let them know about an upcoming event. The purpose of your presentation might be to update everybody at a staff meeting on the progress that each of the company teams is making toward the overall goal of 3,000 phone calls.

Type 4: Selling a Product, Service, or Strategy

■ Sometimes salespeople are given an opportunity to make a sales presentation to a group. But because it's not a one-on-one presentation, they forget it is a sales presentation. They abandon all of the things that they would do in a one-on-one presentation. If the purpose of the presentation is to sell a product or service, the same basic steps must be followed.

Type 5: Obtaining a Decision

■ Your organization is going to have a company outing. Some of the possibilities are a company picnic, a boat cruise, or a day at an amusement park. When giving your recommendation, you may want to list the must-haves and the nice-to-haves for the outing. Then, you can show how each of the possibilities stacks up against the musts and wants. To wind up, you state the preferred option and ask for a decision.

Type 6: Solving a Problem

■ At peak times of the year, your company experiences shipping backlogs beyond what your customers think is reasonable. Your presentation could include stating the problem, presenting facts concerning the problem, identifying causes, stating the ideal outcome, presenting possible solutions, and voicing your recommendations.

2

Knowing the objective of your presentation can be helpful in determining the type of presentation.

Knowing the objective of your presentation can be helpful in determining the type of presentation. For example: If your purpose is to inform, then you are likely to use one of the first three types of presentations—providing information, teaching a skill, or reporting progress. However, if your objective is to persuade, then you would use one of the last three presentation types and persuade by selling a service, product, strategy, or idea; obtaining a decision; or solving a problem.

Take a Moment

List below the last three presentations you have made. Which presentation format could have been used for each presentation?

1._____   _____

2._____   _____

3._____   _____

Outline Formats

Once that you have determined the type of presentation you want to give, you can turn your attention to selecting an outline format. Here are outlines to illustrate each of the six presentation types:

Providing Information

1. Develop a specific purpose statement—a single sentence that tells what your presentation is all about.

2. Decide on an opening.

3. List the information you are going to provide. Generally, try to cover only three to five points. Three points are better than five.

4. Define all acronyms, terms, and jargon.

5. Spell out WII-FM (What's In It For Me). Make the connection between the information and its value to your audience.

6. Close.

For example:

1. Develop a specific purpose statement:

■ Trade shows can be an important new marketing approach for us.

2. Decide on an opening:

■ What would you guess the cost of having a face-to-face contact with a customer or potential customer is right now? (Get two or three responses and post them. Then, explain that trade shows can provide the opportunity to have face-to-face contact with customers at a much lower cost than individual calls.)

3. List information:

1. Our industry has five major trade shows. (List them.)

2. Key people in our company already make presentations at two of them. (List them.)

3. Here are the attendee demographics as well as the costs associated with each trade show. (Show visual.)

4. Here are the hours each show is open and the hours of noncompeting time at each show. (Show visual.)

4. Define jargon, terms, and acronyms:

■ Noncompeting time means that attendees have free time. That is, there are no sessions or other activities scheduled that force attendees to choose between exhibits and some other officially sponsored event.

5. Spell out WII-FM (What's In It For Me).
List the benefits to the audience members or your company:

1. Exhibiting at trade shows increases our visibility to our customers and potential customers.

2. Exhibiting lowers our contact costs by allowing us to determine which prospects warrant follow-up calls.

3. Exhibiting at shows where our company has speakers provides our exhibit with additional credibility.

6. Close:

■ We have the budget to exhibit at three of these shows. We need to develop criteria for choosing which shows to attend.

Take a Moment

Using the format on pages 17 and 18, choose a Providing Information presentation topic and develop an outline by filling in the spaces below.

1. Develop a specific purpose statement.

_____

_____

2. Decide on an opening.

_____

_____

3. List the information you are going to provide.

   1. _____

   2. _____

   3. _____

   4. _____

   5. _____

4. Define all acronyms, terms, and jargon.

_____

_____

5. Spell out WII-FM (What's In It For Me).

_____

_____

6. Close.

_____

_____

Teaching a Skill

1. Answer WII-FM (What's In It For Me) if I learn this skill.

2. Explain the objectives in learning the skill.

3. Show the skill, performing it in its entirety without comment.

4. Show and tell—perform the skill with a running commentary about each step.

5. Have participants practice the skill.

6. Provide feedback so participants know how well they are doing.

7. Review and reinforce the skill. Explain that a skill must be performed three consecutive times with a correct explanation for minimum mastery to take place.

8. Connect the skill to its use back on the job.

9. Answer questions.

10. Have participants plan how they will use the skill on the job.

For example:

■ Your company has installed a new security system.

1. Answer WII-FM (What's In It For Me):

■ Some employees come to work early or stay late. A security system helps to insure their safety. It also safeguards company property when no one is at work.

2. Explain the objectives in learning the skill:

■ We have two objectives today:
   1. To show each of you how to disarm the security system.

   2. To show each of you how to arm the security system when you are on the premises by yourself and when you are leaving the premises unoccupied.

3. Show the skill:

■ Demonstrate the steps without comment for disarming the security system. Then proceed to steps 4 through 10. Later repeat the process for the other two skills.

4. Show and tell:

■ Walk through the steps for disarming the security system, talking through each step as you perform it.

5. Have participants practice the skill:

■ Have each person demonstrate disarming the security system.

6. Provide feedback:

■ Comment on each step as each person performs it, correcting as necessary.

7. Review and reinforce the skill:

■ Instruct each person to disarm the security system at least three times so they have achieved minimum skill mastery.

8. Connect the skill to its use back on the job:

■ Share what happens when the premises are entered without disarming the system. Explain how arming the perimeter provides additional security when employees are working alone. Talk about the consequences of not arming the security system when leaving the premises.

9. Answer questions:

■ Have each person ask one question about anything that you've covered. This can be done separately for each skill.

10. Have participants plan how they will use the skill on the job:

■ Suggest that when employees know they will be the first to enter the building, they recheck their skills the evening before. The same is true for the first time they work late, etc.

Take a Moment

Using the format on pages 20 and 21, choose a Teaching a Skill presentation topic and develop an outline by filling in the spaces below.

1. Answer WII-FM (What's In It For Me).

_____

_____

2. Explain the objectives in learning the skill.

_____

_____

3. Show the skill.

_____

_____

4. Show and tell.

_____

_____

5. Have participants practice the skill.

_____

_____

6. Provide feedback. Then, review and reinforce the skill.

_____

_____

Take a Moment *(continued)*

7. Connect the skill to its use back on the job.

_____

_____

8. Answer questions and have participants plan for use on the job.

_____

_____

2

Reporting Progress

1. Develop a specific purpose statement (a single sentence that tells what your presentation is all about).

2. State the purpose and methodology of the project.

3. Give the status of the project.

4. Give the results of the project to date.

5. List any concerns that have arisen.

6. Suggest or elicit action ideas to resolve the concerns.

7. Define who is responsible for initiating the action steps and set deadlines.

For example:

1. Develop a specific purpose statement:

■ The purpose of this report is to update you on the progress of the "In-Touch" campaign.

2. State the purpose and methodology of the project:

■ We are attempting to contact 3,000 of our most recent clients to inform them of our upcoming 25 percent discount promotion. To achieve this goal, we have divided the company into four teams, which will each make 750 calls.

3. Give the status of the project:

■ Give a status report on each of the teams. Note the calls that remain.

4. Give the results of the project to date:

■ Give the results of the calls that have been made.

5. List any concerns that have arisen:

1. Team members are not fully participating.

2. Calls are not resulting in orders.

3. Too many calls are resulting in leaving voice mail messages that are not being returned.

6. Suggest or elicit action ideas to resolve the concerns.

7. Define who is responsible for initiating the action steps and set deadlines.

Take a Moment

Using the format on pages 23 and 24, choose a Reporting Progress presentation topic and develop an outline by filling in the spaces below.

1. Develop a specific purpose statement (a single sentence that tells what your presentation is all about).

   _____

   _____

2. State the purpose and methodology of the project.

   _____

   _____

3. Give the status of the project.

   _____

   _____

4. Give the results of the project to date.

   _____

   _____

5. List any concerns that have arisen.

   _____

   _____

6. Suggest or elicit action ideas to resolve the concerns.

   _____

   _____

7. Define who is responsible for initiating the action steps and set deadlines.

   _____

Pull the
audience into
your subject.

Selling a Product, Service, or Strategy

1. Get the listener's attention.

2. Maintain the listener's interest.

3. Create desire in the listener.

4. Action Step: We ask the listener to make a buying decision.

For example:

1. **Get the listener's attention.**
   Pull the audience into your subject. People will change or buy in order to avoid pain or gain pleasure. Analyze the audience. In the mind of your audience, what problems or needs does this product satisfy?

   ■ Let's say that a company is continuously hiring new employees who need to use a computer and it can't afford to take weeks to train them to use the computer.

2. **Maintain the listener's interest.**
   What would the value be if we could find a solution to these problems?

   ■ A graphically driven interface like Windows greatly reduces the amount of computer knowledge an employee needs to be able to operate the word processor and spreadsheet programs.

3. **Create desire in the listener.**
   List the features, advantages, and benefits of the product, service, or strategy. Simply put, a feature is what a product, service, or strategy has, an advantage explains what the feature does, and the benefit explains why the feature is important to the customer.

■ Windows provides you with a main menu that allows you to access all applications with a single command. The advantages include:
1. Faster access into any software package.
2. More than one software package can be open at one time.
3. It is easy to move back and forth between all open applications.

The benefits with Windows is that you:
1. Reduce the learning required to start a software program.
2. Reduce the time and work required to leave one software program and move to another.
3. Reduce the time and effort required to move information from one software program to another.

4. Action step:
We ask the listener to make a buying decision.

■ Would you like the training on Windows to be scheduled individually or by department? Or would you prefer installation on Tuesday or Thursday? (An answer to these questions indicate, they have made the choice to buy Windows.)

Take a Moment

Using the format on pages 26 and 27, choose a Selling Product, Service, or Strategy presentation topic and develop an outline by filling in the spaces below.

1. Get the listener's attention.

_____

_____

2. Maintain the listener's interest. What problems or needs does this product satisfy?

_____

_____

3. Create desire in the listener. List the features, advantages, and benefits.

_____

_____

4. Action Step: Ask for the listener to make a buying decision.

_____

_____

Obtaining a Decision

1. Develop a specific purpose statement (a single sentence that tells what your presentation is all about).

2. List the criteria involved in the decision in order of importance. List both must-haves and nice-to-haves.

3. List the alternatives under consideration.

4. Present a comparison of the alternatives, mentioning the positives and negatives for each one. (To obtain the comparison, rate the alternatives according to how well each one meets the criteria.)

5. Recommend one alternative and the action steps for carrying out the decision.

2

For example:

1. Develop a specific purpose statement:

■ We must select a hotel for our company's annual sales meeting.

2. List the criteria involved in the decision in order of importance:

■ These are the criteria we have used in judging the hotels:

Must-have criteria:
1. The hotel must have a meeting room which comfortably holds 300 people.
2. The rental fee for the meeting room can be no more than $500.
3. The hotel must be within 20 minutes driving distance from the airport.

Nice-to-have criteria:
1. Free airport transportation
2. 24-hour room service
3. A swimming pool

3. **List the alternatives under consideration:**

■ Provide a list of hotels.

4. **Present a comparison of the alternatives, mentioning the positives and negatives for each one:**

■ To do this, first rate the hotels according to how well each one meets the criteria:

- All hotels have meeting rooms which will hold 300 people.

- All hotels have rental fees under $500.

- Hotels A and B are five minutes from the airport.

- Hotels C, D, and E are 15 minutes from the airport.

- Hotels C, D, and E are much further from the airport than Hotels A and B so they can be eliminated.

- Hotel A has free airport transportation and 24-hour room service.

- Hotel B has free airport transportation and a swimming pool.

- Because 24-hour room service is more important to us than a swimming pool, Hotel A seems best.

5. **Recommend one alternative and the action steps for carrying out the decision:**

■ I recommend that we make reservations at Hotel A as soon as possible.

Take a Moment

Using the format on pages 29 and 30, choose an Obtaining a Decision presentation topic and develop an outline by filling in the spaces below.

1. Develop a specific purpose statement (a single sentence that tells what your presentation is all about).

_____

_____

2. List the criteria involved in the decision in order of importance. List both must-haves and nice-to-haves.

_____

_____

3. List the alternatives.

_____

_____

4. Rate and compare the alternatives, listing positives and negatives for each.

_____

_____

5. Recommend one alternative and the action steps for carrying out the decision.

_____

_____

Solving a Problem

1. Develop a specific purpose statement (a single sentence that tells what your presentation is all about).

2. Define the problem.

3. List the facts and relevant opinions about the problem.

4. Determine the ideal results to be achieved by solving the problem.

5. List alternatives to solving the problem.

6. Decide which alternatives are most likely to achieve the ideal results.

7. Decide on a solution.

8. Act. Keep in mind that more problems are left unsolved by inaction than by wrong action. With inaction, nothing gets done. With wrong action, you can modify, adjust, adapt, and try again.

For example:

1. Develop a specific purpose statement:

■ The purpose of this meeting is to solve the delayed shipping problems the company experiences in May and October.

2. Define the problem:

■ Our goal is to ship all orders within 48 hours. In May and October, we take an average of 96 hours to ship an order.

3. **List the facts and relevant opinions about the problem:**

■ Most of the year we receive an average of 30 orders per day. During May and October, we receive an average of 60 orders per day. This occurs because of the large catalog mailings we do in March and September.

4. **Determine the ideal results to be achieved by solving the problem:**

■ The ideal result would be shipping all orders within 48 hours.

5. **List alternatives to solving the problem:**

   1. We could hire additional temporary help during the peak times.

   2. We could stagger the catalog mailings so the entire mailing would be dropped over a period of six weeks, rather than at one time.

6. **Decide which alternatives are most likely to achieve the ideal results:**

■ Either will give us the desired result, but staggering will keep us from incurring extra costs.

7. **Decide on a solution to implement:**

■ We will stagger the next catalog mailing over a period of six weeks.

8. **Act:**

■ Our marketing department will develop a new schedule for dropping the mailings.

Take a Moment

Using the format on pages 32 and 33, choose a Solving a Problem presentation topic and develop an outline by filling in the spaces below.

1. Develop a specific purpose statement (a single sentence that tells what your presentation is all about).

   _____

2. Define the problem.

   _____

3. List the facts and relevant opinions about the problem.

   _____

4. Determine the ideal results to be achieved by solving the problem.

   _____

5. List alternatives to solving the problem.

   _____

   _____

6. Decide which alternatives are most likely to achieve the ideal results.

   _____

   _____

7. Decide on a solution.

   _____

8. List an action to be taken.

   _____

Self-Check: Chapter 2 Review

Here are a variety of presentation opportunities. After each one list the format you would use for the presentation. Suggested answers appear on page 90.

2

1. You have to discuss excessive personal phone calls on company time at an executive team meeting. (You are a member of the executive team.)

   _____

2. You have to update the company at an all-company meeting on the status of the company's profit-sharing plan.

   _____

3. You have to make a presentation to a customer on the advantages of upgrading the latest model of your product.

   _____

4. You must make a presentation to the executive team on three employee incentive plans you have researched. The goal is to implement one.

   _____

5. You must show four employees how to use the company's on-line order entry system.

   _____

Chapter *Three*

Organizing and Preparing Your Presentation

Chapter Objectives

▶ Understand the basic concepts of MindMapping.

▶ Be able to select from six formats for organizing content.

MindMapping

When I use MindMapping, it reduces the time it takes me to develop a presentation, a report, an article, or a letter by approximately 50 percent.

ne of the greatest challenges when making presentations is preparing for them. Many people sit down, they pick up a sheet of paper, and their minds go blank. They don't know where to start. Or they have so many ideas they don't know how to organize them. Or they don't have enough information to choose a format or decide on the points to be covered.

I have read a book called *Use Both Sides of Your Brain* by Tony Buzan that I feel is very helpful in putting presentations on the right track. A significant part of the book outlines a technique which Tony calls MindMapping. When I use MindMapping, it reduces the time it takes me to develop a presentation, a report, an article, or a letter by approximately 50 percent. Mind-Mapping allows me to use words to visually relate concepts and information in ways that are more enlightening than note taking or outlining.

MindMapping a presentation helps me to take a look at how I may want to present the information. It enables me to focus not only on the content, but also on the sequence of the content. On pages 38 and 39 is a mind map that I created in 10 minutes for this book. A mind map helps me to see not only what is there, but also what is missing.

36

Here are the fundamental aspects of MindMapping:

◆ **Start with your central thought.**
Write this premise in the middle of a blank sheet of paper. Then, list the first support idea that comes into your mind in the 12:00 position. Next, note any related points. As you exhaust ideas on a topic, move to the 1:00 position and begin again. Continue around the clock.

◆ **Be free-flowing.**
One of the models that I use for the mind looks like a pinball machine. It can bounce around very quickly to numerous ideas before it comes up with a logical conclusion. We've all had this experience: Someone says something to you. You pause for a minute and then reply. Your listener asks where in the world your response came from. You reply, "You said this, which reminded me of that, and that made me think of that, which reminded me of that, and that's why I said that to you." For you, the thought progression was very logical, but anyone else looking at it can't see how you got from the original statement to your reply. The Mind-Mapping technique accommodates this type of bouncing around better than either note taking or outlining.

◆ **Use only key words.**
Often when taking notes and creating an outline, we use too many words. Most people think faster than they write. (The human mind can think 1,200 to 1,600 words a minute. On average, most people only write freehand 25 to 35 words a minute, and the best of us can type little more than 100 words a minute.) So the key concept is to think in bullets and jot down one or two words that capture the concept. This way you won't slow down your thinking.

The key concept is to think in bullets and jot down one or two words that capture the concept.

3

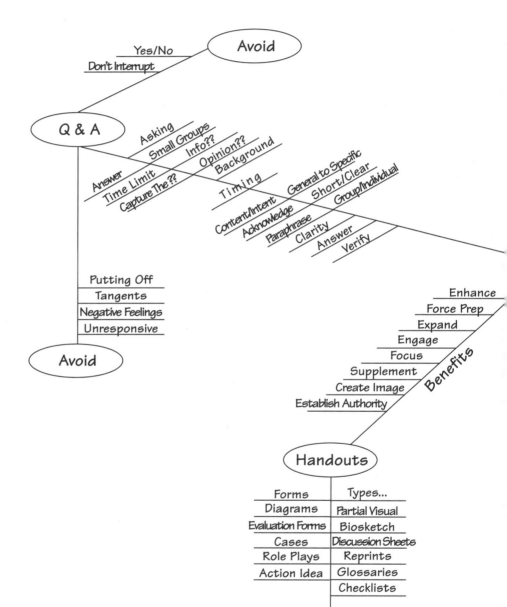

Avoid

Yes/No
Don't Interrupt

Q & A

Asking
Small Groups
Info??
Opinion??
Background
Answer
Time Limit
Capture The??
Timing
Content/Intent
General to Specific
Short/Clear
Group/Individual
Acknowledge
Paraphrase
Clarity
Answer
Verify

Putting Off
Tangents
Negative Feelings
Unresponsive

Avoid

Enhance
Force Prep
Expand
Engage
Focus
Supplement
Create Image
Establish Authority

Benefits

Handouts

Forms	Types...
Diagrams	Partial Visual
Evaluation Forms	Biosketch
Cases	Discussion Sheets
Role Plays	Reprints
Action Idea	Glossaries
	Checklists

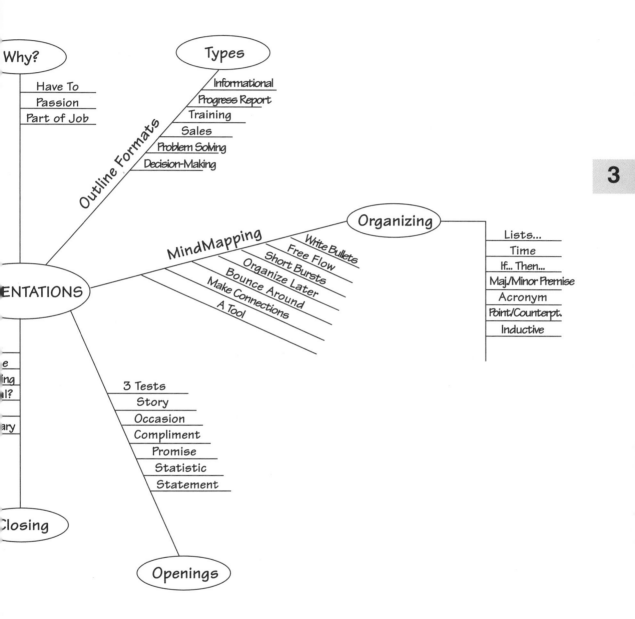

Why?
- Have To
- Passion
- Part of Job

Types
- Informational
- Progress Report
- Training
- Sales
- Problem Solving
- Decision-Making

Outline Formats

Organizing
- Lists...
- Time
- If... Then...
- Maj./Minor Premise
- Acronym
- Point/Counterpt.
- Inductive

MindMapping
- White Bullets
- Free Flow
- Short Bursts
- Organize Later
- Bounce Around
- Make Connections
- A Tool

ENTATIONS

e
ing
l?

ary

- 3 Tests
- Story
- Occasion
- Compliment
- Promise
- Statistic
- Statement

Closing

Openings

◆ **Allow yourself to bounce around.**
It may be that you get to the third or fourth key idea and suddenly you think of something that fits back with idea number one. That's O.K.—stop, bounce back up, add the idea, and continue on.

◆ **Feel free to connect things that relate.**
When two topics relate to one another, simply draw an arrow to connect them. The arrow may be drawn with the same color as the rest of the mind map or with another color to highlight clearly the intended connection.

◆ **Try short bursts.**
Time yourself for five minutes. Then, take a break. Sit back. Look at your mind map. Do something else. Then, spend another five minutes adding, modifying, and adjusting.

◆ **Use MindMapping alone or in groups.**
See page 47 for an example of a mind map for a Creative Training Techniques seminar that a group of participants produced in 20 minutes to summarize what they had learned in the seminar.

Remember, MindMapping is your tool. Let it work for you. Many people, when exposed to MindMapping, say, "I could never show this to my boss." A mind map is not necessarily for others. Rather, it is primarily for yourself. Don't use a mind map as a report. Instead, use the mind map to dictate or type the report. Use it to make sure that all the elements you want in the report are there before you start.

Take a Moment

On a separate piece of paper, construct a mind map, using the MindMapping process that has just been presented, for a presentation that you will most likely be giving in the next few months.

Organizing a Presentation

Once you know all the content that you want to cover, how do you want to organize it? Try one of the following organizing methods. When choosing a method, always keep in mind your objective. Ask yourself: Will this sequencing method help me (and my audience) reach my objective?

> **When choosing a method, always keep in mind your objective.**

The List Approach

If you have a number of points to make that seem to be about equal in importance with no particular priority, simply make a list. If you do this, however, don't number the points because numbers indicate sequence or priority. Instead, simply use bullets. For example:

- Here are three things that you need to succeed in business:
  - Do good.
  - Have fun.
  - Make money.

Do these three steps have a sequence? Some might say you need to make money first. Others might say if you do good the money will come. However, if you do good and make money, but you are not having fun, what is the point? So all three are about equal in importance. It is important to do good in business. It also is important that you have fun along the way, and the bottom line is that you can't continue in business if you are not making money.

Chronological Sequence

This format uses time to create the order of presentation. For example:

■ We are having a conference in the third quarter of this year:
   A. Here are the things that need to happen in the first quarter.
   B. Here are the things that need to happen in the second quarter.
   C. Here's what needs to happen in the third quarter for the conference to be a success.

Another chronological organizing option is past, present, and future. This method is easy to use, especially for impromptu presentations. For example:

■ In the past, I have used two types of visuals—single-color overhead transparencies and flip charts. In the present, I not only continue to use overheads and flip charts, but I have added full-color transparencies generated on a color printer. I also use computer images in my presentations. In the future, I see adding animation and sound clips to the computer images.

Acronyms

Sometimes you can create an acronym to aid in remembering the sequence of points in the body of the presentation. For example:

■ As a pastor I used the theme:
   If you really care, **SHARE**.

   S-how you have benefitted.
   H-ave the attitude of a learner.
   A-cquire a backlog of experiences—not only how you have been helped, but how others have been helped, too.
   R-emember to build the principles into your life—because what you do speaks so loudly that I can't hear what you say.
   E-mphasize that everyone can benefit.

The acronym helped me to remember the sequence of points to be presented and provided a tool to help my audience readily recall the points for themselves.

Chain of Reasoning

This pattern provides a series of points that logically flow from one to another, like links in a chain. Here are two examples:

■ To be a balanced person you must have goals in six areas of life—spiritual, mental, physical, social, financial, and family.

■ The three parts to an effective golf stroke are grip, setup, and swing.

Point/Counterpoint

This is used to present contrasting viewpoints. For example:

■ A move to a new space would positively impact our production capacity (point), but negatively impact our cash flow (counterpoint).

Inductive/Deductive Reasoning

Inductive reasoning takes a series of facts and draws a conclusion from them. For example:

Fact:
Technology is changing the way people do their jobs.

Fact:
Training is needed to prepare people to use new technology.

Fact:
The average adult is retrained three times in his or her working career.

Conclusion:
Training will continue to play an important role in industry.

3

Inductive reasoning takes a series of facts and draws a conclusion from them.

Deductive reasoning takes a major premise or general principle, adds a fact or an example, and draws a conclusion from it.

Deductive reasoning takes a major premise or general principle, adds a fact or an example, and draws a conclusion from it. Using this method successfully requires that you be very careful about the validity of your major premise. Here is an example:

Major premise:
When the company does well, we stop controlling our expenses.

Fact:
We are currently doing well.

Conclusion:
We are not controlling our expenses.

Notice that the strength and weakness of this approach is in the truthfulness of the major premise. Is it really true that every time the company does well, we stop controlling our expenses?

Here's another example:

Major premise:
Avoiding foods with high fat content will lower your cholesterol.

Fact:
I am avoiding foods with high fat content.

Conclusion:
I am lowering my cholesterol.

This one is better, but it still has a flaw. Avoiding foods with high fat content is one factor in reducing cholesterol. Another is regular aerobic exercise. If I start avoiding foods with high fat content but discontinue my regular exercise program, it is possible that my cholesterol could increase.

Putting It All Together

MindMapping can help you come up with the points you want to cover in your presentation. Using one or more of the sequences listed in this chapter to organize your presentation can make it easier for your listeners to follow your presentation. It can also increase their acceptance of your content.

MindMapping can help you come up with the points you want to cover in your presentation.

Take a Moment

Referring to the mind map that you created earlier in this chapter, use one or more of the seven organization methods to sequence your presentation.

3

_____

_____

_____

_____

_____

_____

_____

_____

Self-Check: Chapter 3 Review

Indicate True or False for each of the statements below. Suggested answers are given on page 90.

_____ 1. MindMapping can help cut presentation preparation time.

_____ 2. Writing bullet phrases helps keep ideas flowing.

_____ 3. You must be artistic to use MindMapping.

_____ 4. A series of events to be reported would lend itself to a chronological approach.

_____ 5. A list is a good way to organize points of about equal importance.

_____ 6. Acronyms do not help people remember your main points.

3

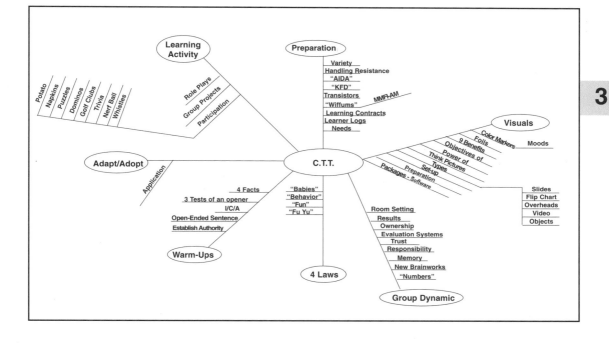

Chapter *Four*

Opening and Closing Your Presentation

Chapter Objectives

▶ List the three tests of an effective opening.

▶ Select an opening to use in one of your own presentations.

▶ Select a closing to use in one of your own presentations.

Opening a Presentation Effectively

The opening to your presentation should break the listeners' preoccupation and get them involved.

Sometimes a speaker giving a presentation doesn't really open; he or she just starts, and often that start is slow and rambling. To make sure your opening is effective, ask yourself these three questions:

◆ **Does the opening break preoccupation?**
   Just because people are physically in a room for a presentation doesn't mean that they are mentally ready to listen. They may be wondering whether or not this meeting is worth their time. They may be thinking about work left undone. They may be thinking about a problem at home. To capture your audience, the opening to your presentation should break the listeners' preoccupation and get them involved.

◆ **Does the opening facilitate networking?**
When people come into a presentation, they may feel insecure and be asking themselves a number of questions. Will I fit? Will I know as much as everyone else? Will I be able to make a contribution? Is anything going to happen that's going to make me look stupid? When listeners are tense or ill at ease, their retention goes down. The faster you can get people to feel at ease with one another and with the situation, the more open they will be to the information you share.

◆ **Is the opening relevant to the presentation?**
Whatever type of opening you use, make sure that it is relevant. Often a presenter will choose an icebreaker from a book to open. Does the icebreaker use involvement? Yes. Does it facilitate networking by getting people to talk to one another? Probably yes. Is it relevant? Frequently no. It leaves the listeners asking: What is the point? The point is, there is no point. Besides wasting time, an irrelevant opener may leave your listeners wondering if the presentation is worth their time.

> **The faster you can get people to feel at ease with one another and with the situation, the more open they will be to the information you share.**

4

Types of Openings

There are numerous ways to get a presentation off to a good start. Here are eight of the best types of openings you might want to consider for your next presentation.

Tell a Story

People generally like stories. However, the story opening can be even more impressive and have greater impact if you involve your audience in the story. Here is an example:

■ Imagine that you are 28 years old and working very hard in an organization. Last Friday you were promoted to vice president. You are now one of three vice presidents. As a result of your promotion, you have nine managers who report to you.

During your four years with the company, you have worked with all of these people at one time or another. On Monday you meet with each of them individually. One by one each person indirectly implies that you really are the best person for the job. Each person also tells you that he or she is glad that you got the promotion and is looking forward to being part of your team because you deliver results.

So now it is Tuesday. You are about to have your first staff meeting. You are in your new office. It not only has room for your work space, but it also has a conference table large enough for your nine managers and yourself. You come to work that day wearing a blue blazer. If you are a man, you are wearing red golf slacks. If you are a woman, you are wearing a red skirt. You begin the meeting. You are creating a vision, setting goals, and looking at the future of your team. Things are really exciting. The president of your company steps into your office. He looks at you from head to toe, and looks at you again, and then looks one more time. Finally, he says, pointing a finger at you, "You—get up. Get out of here. Leave this building. Go home and do not come back until you are dressed like a professional." Then, the president waits until you stand up, leave the conference table, leave your managers, leave your office, and exit the building.

As you slide into your car and look up at your office window, you see the president looking down at you. Let me ask: How do you feel?

You will notice that the story is not about another person or about the speaker. The story puts each audience member right in the picture. The story makes audience members feel this experience has happened to them.

Refer to the Occasion

Maybe there is something significant about the occasion surrounding your presentation. If so, it might make a very effective way to open. When you use this approach, make sure you involve your audience. Most presenters don't. They will say something like: This is a very special occasion. It is the 10th anniversary of our company. The audience thinks: So what?

Here's how you might bring involvement to this type of opening. I recently spoke to the British Columbia (Canada) Emergency Preparedness Conference. It was the fifth annual conference. As I opened my keynote presentation, I said:

■ Today is a very significant day. It's significant for two reasons. One of them you already know—it's the fifth anniversary of this conference.

   There also is something even more significant about today that should be acknowledged. In your small groups (I had the audience arranged at tables of six to eight), I will give you 30 seconds to brainstorm your best guess as to what else is significant about today. You have 30 seconds. Go.

Thirty seconds later, I got a number of guesses about what else was so significant. After six or seven guesses, I said:

■ I really am glad that you recognize so many significant things about this conference, but there is one thing that hasn't been mentioned. Most of you are not aware of it. You see, this could very easily be the 10th anniversary of this conference. The original planning committee for this conference worked for five years before they were able to get the support and funding to do this conference the first time.

   Each successive year since the first conference, there has been standing room only at these conferences. People are turned away. There is a pressing need for this conference, yet it took dedicated people five years of ongoing commitment to be successful the first time. I think the original planning committee as well as the successive planning committees should be acknowledged for their persistence and for their commitment to excellence.

4

I then asked attendees who had been part of any planning committee to stand, and the audience acknowledged them with their applause.

Offer a Sincere Compliment

People appreciate compliments if they are sincere. However, to gain involvement, try turning the compliment into a question. For example: You are running a customer service meeting. You start your presentation by saying:

> **People appreciate compliments if they are sincere.**

■ The group assembled in this room really deserves to be congratulated. You know from our last meeting that the three most significant customer complaints that we received were:
   1. Errors in packing orders.
   2. Delays in shipping beyond our promise of shipping within 48 hours.
   3. Materials being received in damaged condition.

Each of those customer service complaints has dropped significantly. I will give you one minute in your small groups to give me your best guess as to how significant the drop has been in those three areas. To refresh your memory, the last period we had 60 complaints about shipping errors, 48 complaints about late shipments, and 37 complaints about materials received in damaged condition.

After the audience has a minute to discuss the subject, you get guesses from various groups, and now the springboard is set for you to present the following information:

■ Shipping errors dropped from 60 to 40—a 33 percent improvement. Here are the things you did to make that happen . . .

Late shipments dropped from 48 to 24—a 50 percent improvement. Here is what you did to make that happen . . .

Materials received in damaged condition dropped from 37 to 12—a 66 percent improvement. Here's what you did to make that happen . . .

Start with a Quotation

4

Even with this type of opening, give first consideration to getting the audience involved. For example, if you are doing a presentation on creativity, you might say: "Who said, 'Imagination is more important than knowledge'?" Allow the audience in groups of twos or threes to come up with a guess. After the groups share their guesses, you reveal that the author was Albert Einstein—a perfect lead into creativity.

Make a Significant Statement

A significant statement can get the audience's immediate attention. For example, you are making a sales presentation to a group that is making a decision on your product. You start by saying something like: "There are three significant features available exclusively with our product—features that provide you with tremendous benefits." Your presentation can then delineate the three features along with the specific benefits that your prospects will receive.

A significant statement can get the audience's immediate attention.

Refer to the Previous Speaker

Often presenters are unaware of what previous presenters have said. Sometimes presenters duplicate and contradict one another. This can be embarrassing if you are from the same organization and should be complementing one another. Whenever possible, incorporate previous presenters into your opening.

Here is one way I used this technique effectively. I was delivering the morning general session at a conference. I started by saying:

■ How many of you were here for the opening session last night? What an impressive opening! Nothing gets the adrenaline flowing like a drum and bugle corps. I also was impressed by your opening speaker. Two of the most important things he said were: learn something new about your industry every day and find one way you can improve on your job every day. My goal this morning is for you to leave this session with at least five ways to improve your next presentation. This will help you to improve in at least one area of your job.

Notice that I actually combined three openings here. I paid a compliment. I referred to a statement of a previous speaker which told the audience I cared enough to be involved in their event. Finally, I made a promise—which is the next technique for opening.

Make a Promise

This can be as simple as saying: "By the end of this presentation, you'll have at least five ways you can create a more motivational environment for your employees. None of these will require pay, promises, or promotions."

> **Whenever possible, incorporate previous presenters into your opening.**

Ask a Challenging Question

Here is an example: In one presentation I talk about the 10 deadly sins of presentations. (For you, the subject could be the 10 deadly sins of customer service, closing sales, quality improvement, etc.) I start my speech like this:

■ Over the past five years, I've asked more than 22,000 people for the worst things they've ever seen in a presentation— things that really turned them off and tuned them out. Today I'm going to share with you their top 10. Before I do, though, I'd like you to brainstorm your top 10 and we'll see how they compare. In your small groups, brainstorm the 10 worst things you've seen a presenter do.

When the brainstorming time is over, I have each group share one idea. I then share my top 10 starting from number 10 in the same way David Letterman does. This technique keeps the listeners involved, comparing their top 10 to my list to see how many match.

Remember—your entire presentation will be judged by the way that you open. People will continue to listen or will stop listening as a result of what you say and do in the first few minutes.

4

Your entire presentation will be judged by the way you open.

Take a Moment

Think about one presentation you need to give. Choose one of the openings that have just been discussed and write below how you would use it in your presentation.

_____

_____

_____

Closing a Presentation Effectively

Closing is another critical part of your presentation. Just as people open ineffectively, some never close at all. They just run out of time. The guidelines for an effective closing are not as cut and dried as for opening, but consider these:

Make sure your closing ties things together.

◆ Make sure your closing ties things together. Many presentation and training programs don't wrap up. They just stop.

◆ For many types of presentations, action planning is appropriate. If you've given people ideas and information you want them to act upon, make sure that you allow them time to plan for how they'll apply the information and use the skills. If there's no time to reflect on application during the presentation, the chances are there will be little opportunity afterwards.

◆ Whenever appropriate, allow time for celebration as a part of the close. Many presentations provide opportunities for people to change and grow. People leave knowing things they didn't know before. They are able to do things they couldn't do before. They leave with more confidence in their own abilities. They've made difficult decisions or solved serious problems. They leave having provided useful input. All of these are reasons to celebrate.

Take a Moment

As you think over one of your past presentations, what did people gain in terms of knowledge or new skills? What did they provide by way of input? What problems did they solve? List these below. They are all reasons to celebrate!

_____

_____

_____

_____

4

Types of Closings

Here are five types of closings to consider to give a sense of completeness to your presentations:

◆ **Summarize.**
If you have time, you might want to divide your audience into small groups of no more than five. Ask them to take 90 seconds to reflect on the presentation and list ideas they have for future action. Then, give them an additional three minutes to share their action ideas within the small groups. Finally, go from group to group, asking each to share one of its action ideas. Depending on your audience size, you might do this just once per group or several times. During each part of this closing, people will find themselves adding to their action ideas, and the presentation will end with them feeling that they've received a great deal of value.

◆ **Recap.**
If your time is shorter, you might choose to recap key points or action ideas for your audience.

◆ **Tell an anecdote.**
An *anecdote* is a story about someone else. For a sales presentation, you might close by sharing an anecdote about a previous customer who made the same buying decision as the current customer is making. As part of the story, list the specific benefits the previous customer received in the weeks and months since the decision. In a training presentation, you might close with an anecdote about a recent participant, explaining how applying the skills and knowledge learned in the presentation have helped in his or her job.

◆ **Ask a rhetorical question.**
A *rhetorical question* is one you want the members of the audience to think about but that you are not expecting them to respond to out loud. For example, let's say you were leading an informational meeting about your company's retirement plan, trying to encourage employees to voluntarily contribute to the plan. The audience is made up of people in their 20s and early 30s. They see retirement as a very distant thing—nothing they need to plan for now. After sharing all the information, you close by saying:

Your audience should think about a rhetorical question, but not answer out loud.

■ According to statistics, most people at age 65 are either dead, dead broke, or dependent on friends or relatives for support. Less than 5 percent can take care of themselves financially. How many of us have parents or grandparents who are at or near retirement age? How many of them are free to live the lifestyle they choose because they have put aside enough money for their retirement? If they have not saved for retirement, how do you think they feel after working all their lives that they must hope that someone else will take care of them? By taking advantage of the company's retirement plan, you and I can insure that we will never be in a position where we must hope that someone else has the resources to take care of us. We will have the resources to take care of ourselves.

Note that no one is really expected to volunteer an answer to these questions. Nor will they discuss them in small groups. Rather, the questions are designed as rhetorical ones— questions for the members of the audience to think about without necessarily sharing their answers.

◆ **End like the beginning.**
This is a favorite closing device of Paul Harvey on his national radio program. At the beginning of a broadcast, he gives information about a person, a situation, or an action. Then he moves to other topics. At the end of his broadcast, he comes back to the first story and says something like: "Remember the little guy who . . . ?" He then concludes by saying: "Well he grew up to be . . ." The person is usually some famous personality. Paul Harvey concludes by saying, "And that's the rest of the story—good day."

Here's another example. It is an effective conclusion to the presentation that began with the members of the audience imagining themselves being promoted to vice presidents and wearing red golf slacks or red skirts to work that we alluded to at the beginning of this chapter.

■ Well, in 1972 I was promoted to vice president. I wore red golf slacks along with a blue blazer. I was sent home. That day, I learned more about how I will and will not treat people at work than on any day before or since. What the president said wasn't wrong, but when and how he said it—in my opinion— were. How are you and I going to lead and work with the people assigned to us? Will our employees learn from us as a positive example? Or, are they going to say, "I'll never treat someone that way!"? The choice is yours and mine to make every day. Let's make the choice a good one. And that's the rest of the story. Good day!

4

Take a Moment

Review the closings that have just been discussed and then modify, adjust, or adapt one of them for a presentation you want to make.

_____

_____

_____

_____

Remember, by creating and using a high-impact opening as well as a high-impact closing, you reinforce the value of your message a hundredfold.

Self-Check: Chapter 4 Review

Indicate True or False for each of the statements below.
Suggested answers are given on page 90.

_____1. Breaking audience preoccupation is an important test
of any opening.

_____2. Audience involvement is the key to breaking
preoccupation.

_____3. Presentations of less than 15 minutes in length don't
require an opening.

_____4. Not every presentation requires a closing.

_____5. Action planning can be an important part of closing.

_____6. One important consideration for a closing is that it
ties things together.

4

Chapter *Five*

Asking and Answering Questions

Chapter Objectives

▶ Use the technique of asking questions to involve your entire audience.

▶ Ask questions effectively.

▶ Identify why traditional ways of asking for questions often fail.

▶ Answer questions effectively.

Perfecting the skill of asking and answering questions can add depth and interest to your presentation.

Perfecting the skill of asking and answering questions can add depth and interest to your presentation. Both techniques are effective ways to involve your audience in what you have to say. This chapter will help you understand how questions can work for you.

Asking Questions to Involve Your Audience

Asking questions is one of the best ways to keep an audience actively involved in a presentation. A technique I use frequently is to divide my audience into small groups to discuss questions. This is far better than asking a general question that anyone, including the most vocal audience members, can answer. This technique allows for more audience interaction and avoids the challenge of having a few vocal people dominate the presentation.

Here is how I use the technique. I begin by saying,

■ Here is a question I would like your small group to discuss. Once I have asked the question, I will give you a minute to discuss your answer. Then, I will ask two or three groups to volunteer their responses. Here is the question: What do you think are the three most significant causes of customer complaints in our organization? You have 60 seconds in your small groups.

At the end of 60 seconds, I ask one group for an answer, another group for a second answer, and another group for a third. I post these on a flip chart or on an overhead. Then, I compare the responses to data from the company.

Tips on Asking Questions

As you use this question-and-answer technique in your presentations, remember these key points:

5

1. **Plan your questions.**
   Think through the questions you will ask. Decide at what point in your presentation you will ask them.

2. **Distinguish between two kinds of questions: One is to get information, and the second is to get opinions.**
   Answers to information questions are either right or wrong. For example, the question "What is the company's policy on immediate termination?" has a right or wrong answer, while the question "What do you think are the three most common sources of customer complaints?" does not. In the second case, I'm asking the person what he or she thinks or feels. I'm asking for an opinion. Opinions are neither right nor wrong. They are simply opinions.

3. **Make sure you relate the question to the audience's background.**

   To understand your question, your audience needs a frame of reference. For example, you are giving a sales presentation to a small company considering the purchase of cellular phones for key employees. You might say:

> To understand your question, your audience needs a frame of reference.

■ One concern raised by small companies getting into cellular phones for the first time is that the phones become toys rather than tools. A decision like this needs to be made for business reasons. I'd like to suggest five business reasons for using cellular phones. As I list each of them, I'd like you to rate the importance of the reason to yourself and to the business. We'll use a five-point scale with 1 signifying no importance and 5 representing high importance. Here's the list: One—being in touch at critical times. For example, one client was on his way to an important business presentation. An accident backed up the freeway. It took him 30 minutes to get to a phone. He arrived an hour late with 90 people waiting. The client said that it only took this happening to him once to realize that the cost of a cellular phone for a year would have been repaid many times over by being able to reach the client while he was stuck on the freeway.

After sharing the five reasons, you ask which of the business reasons were rated the highest. Then each person shares his or her response.

4. **As you ask questions, go from the general to the specific.**
   For example, if you are doing an employee orientation, you might say:

■ In what section of the employee manual do we find the policies about vacation? I will give you 30 seconds in your small group.

Notice this is an information question. There is a right or wrong answer, and because it is employee orientation, you can't assume that everyone will know. So instead, give them permission to use a resource to make sure the answer they give is correct. Once they find the section, you might ask a more specific question, such as: "What is the company's policy concerning taking vacation before your first anniversary?" Notice this question narrows the focus. The answer is a subset of the overall company policy on vacations.

5. **Stick to one topic at a time.**
   For example, when asking questions about the vacation policy, stick to the vacation policy. When you are finished, move on to sick days. Don't bounce back and forth.

6. **Make sure that your questions are short and clear.**
   Consider putting the questions on an overhead transparency so they are clearly visible. I once heard a person say,

5

■ There are six steps to the problem-solving process:
   1. Identify the problem.
   2. Collect facts and opinions.
   3. Determine your ideal solution.
   4. Brainstorm alternatives.
   5. Considering the alternatives in step 4, pick the combination most likely to give your ideal result in step 3.
   6. Act.

   Which step do you think causes people the most trouble?

Because the question was asked verbally and a copy of it did not appear on the overhead projector, most of the audience was lost by the time the speaker got to the end of the question. If I were going to ask a question such as that, I would say:

■ On the overhead projector, you will see the six steps to the problem-solving process. Here they are. In your small groups, please discuss this question: Which of these steps do you think causes people the most trouble?

With the steps visible, the audience members don't have to remember the steps of the problem-solving process, and they can focus on your question.

7. **Make logical transitions between questions.**
For example, "Now that we've answered the questions that relate to Step 1 in the problem-solving process, let's consider questions concerning Step 2." Or, "Now that we've talked about the process we used to arrive at our decision, let's consider questions about implementation."

8. **If you are not using the small-group approach to elicit answers, ask questions of the group first.**
Then select individuals to respond. For example, even though you plan to call on Susan, ask the question of the whole group and make eye contact with everyone in the room. This way, if you see that you are not getting good eye contact from Susan, but you are getting nods from several other people, you can choose one of them, rather than putting Susan on the spot. Asking a question directly of one person causes other parts of the audience to tune out.

> Asking a question directly of one person causes other parts of the audience to tune out.

9. **Avoid yes, no, or answer-implied questions.**
Questions like, "The employees don't mind working overtime, do they?" is an answer-implied question with the implication being, "No, they don't." Or, "Group involvement is important, isn't it?" (The implied answer is "Yes.") "Is today a special day?" (Here the answer is "Yes" or "No," but if the answer is "Yes," we still have no idea why the day is important.)

10. **Once you have asked a question, don't interrupt.**
Let the other person answer. Give the person the opportunity to provide his or her response to your question.

> Once you
> have asked
> a question,
> don't interrupt.
> Let the other
> person answer.

Answering Questions to Reinforce Your Message

Including a question-and-answer session as part of a presentation is a good way to clear up any confusion in the minds of audience members, and it gives you the chance to restate the key points of your message.

5

Two Common Q & A Mistakes

Asking for and answering questions can add energy and interest to just about any presentation. Yet, handling Q & A sessions is something that quite often trips up presenters. They make two common mistakes. They ask for questions in the wrong way and at the wrong time.

1. **Soliciting questions in the wrong way**

   You may wonder how a presenter can ask for questions in the wrong way. Here's how. A speaker finishes a presentation and says, "Now before I go, are there any questions?" There are two problems with this approach. First, the speaker may not get any questions. Or, second, there may be an audience member who will take issue with points in the presentation and use the Q & A time, not to ask questions, but to present his or her viewpoints. I find the best question-and-answer approach is to say:

   ■ Let's take about 10 minutes for questions and answers. Get in small groups of three or four. You have two minutes to brainstorm one or two questions you would like to ask about anything we have covered so far.

   After about 90 seconds, I ask for a group to volunteer to ask the first question. I answer that question and have that group choose the next group to ask a question. I also ask someone to be timekeeper. I answer as many questions as I can until the 10 minutes are up.

   I then say:

   ■ I know you have other questions. Feel free to do one of two things: One—check with me at the break, and I will be happy to give a one-on-one answer. Or two—I have a capture-the-question flip chart posted on the wall here. Write your question on a Post-it and stick it on the flip chart. I will look over the questions and work in answers during the presentation.

This approach offers several advantages:

◆ It gives people a chance to think about their questions.

◆ It allows the members of the audience to build on one another's questions and clarify them.

◆ Some of the questions may be answered by the audience members themselves. This insures the questions asked are more likely to be of greater interest to the audience.

◆ It involves more people in the Q & A process.

2. **Asking for questions at the wrong time**
Timing is everything when it comes to asking for questions. Many presenters will say, "Before we go on break, are there any questions?" or "Before we leave for the day, are there any questions?" Who wants to be the person that keeps the rest of the group from going on break, or to lunch, or home? They may have questions, but they're unlikely to ask them.

The best times to ask for questions are at least 20 minutes before any scheduled break and well before the end of the day. Better yet, do a Q & A session after people have come back from a break.

> **Timing is everything when it comes to asking for questions.**

5

Tips for Answering Questions

Answering questions is not just a matter of starting to talk. I have found that audiences will get much more out of a Q & A session if you follow this approach.

1. **Listen to both the content (what is said) and the intent (what is meant).**
All too often we do a great job of listening for the content, but fail to pick up the intent, or the feelings and emotions, behind the question. Take, for example, the question, "This session does end at 4:30, doesn't it?" The content is a request for the ending time of the presentation, but the voice inflection and word emphasis say that the intent is to make it clear that the presentation had better end by then. However, with the question "Does this session really end at 4:30?" the voice inflection could indicate that the speaker wishes the presentation would go beyond 4:30.

2. **Acknowledge the question.**
   Say: "I appreciate your asking that."

3. **Paraphrase the question.**
   Say: "Let me see if I understand what you are asking. What you're asking is . . ." Repeat the question, but use different words. For example, someone might ask, "Which is more important, quality or service?" My response would be:

   ■ That's a good question (acknowledgment). Let me make sure I understand what you are asking. What you are asking is—given an option of quality or service, which would I choose as being most important? Is that your question?

   Notice that I acknowledged the question and paraphrased it. Finally, I got agreement from the person that I have understood the question.

4. **If necessary, ask for clarification.**
   There may be times that you are asked a question and you do not understand it. Simply ask for clarification. For example, I once had someone ask me, "How do you deal with a boss who won't let you apply what you have learned in a training program back on the job?" This is a pretty broad question. So I said, "That's a good question. To make sure I understand what you are looking for, could you give me an example?" I did this because there could be a number of reasons why a boss might not support application of training. Rather than getting into numerous issues, I would rather focus on the one issue the questioner has in mind.

5. **Answer the question briefly, yet completely.**

6. **Verify.**
   I always want people to acknowledge that I have answered a question. So when I finish answering the question, I will say, "Was that helpful?" or "Did I say enough about that?" or "Is that what you were looking for?"

Pitfalls When Answering Questions

I have just gone over the best approach for answering questions, but there are some pitfalls to avoid when answering questions. Here are four:

1. **Avoid being unresponsive.**
   For example, when a participant raises his or her hand for the 50th time, and you say, "Well, if there aren't any other questions, let's move on," you are being unresponsive in ignoring the person. Even though this person may have asked far too many questions, the group still may feel that you have not lived up to the standard they expect from a presenter.

2. **Don't show your negative feelings.**
   When Joe Jerk has asked his 75th question, don't sigh, look at the ceiling, look at the floor, and say, "You have another question, Joe?" in a tone that reflects your exasperation. Also, avoid comments that indicate a question is stupid such as, "Fred, if you had been paying attention, you would know that I just covered that 10 minutes ago."

5

3. **Don't delay answering questions.**
   Whenever possible, try to answer questions when they are asked. The only exception is when answering the question would confuse more audience members than it would help. Then, say something like:

> **Try to answer questions when they are asked.**

■ Chris, that's a great question, but in order to give an answer that is helpful for the entire group, I need to lay some groundwork. So, please write the question on a Post-it and put it on the capture-the-question board. I need about an hour to lay the groundwork for the entire group. If I have not answered your question within an hour, would you then bring it up again?

This way Chris knows that I am not trying to bury the question and that I do commit to coming back to it. This technique also allows me to cover the information needed so that all of the audience members can benefit from the answer.

4. **Avoid tangents.**
   Some illustrative stories are helpful, but not all. One of the worst things a speaker can do is to constantly be saying, "That reminds me of a time when . . . " and then go off on a 10-minute tangent. When the presenter comes back to the question, no one really knows where the discussion has been and very few people care. And at the end of the tangent, the audience doesn't even remember what the question was that generated the story in the first place.

By understanding how to ask and answer questions properly, you will be well on your way to providing a valuable, professional presentation.

Self-Check: Chapter 5 Review

Indicate True or False for each of the statements below. Suggested answers are given on page 91.

_____1. An ideal time to ask for questions is just before a break.

_____2. It is important to ask general questions first, then more specific questions.

_____3. When someone asks a question, make sure you listen for both the content and the intent.

_____4. Paraphrasing a person's question before answering it helps to insure that you understand the question.

_____5. Asking "Are there any questions?" is a good way to begin a Q & A session.

_____6. Sticking to a time limit for a Q & A session means that some people won't get their questions answered.

_____7. A capture-the-question board allows shy people to post questions without being forced to ask them in front of the whole group.

5

Chapter *Six*

Using Handouts in Your Presentation

Chapter Objectives

▶ Understand eight reasons why handouts are important to a presentation.

▶ Select at least two types of handout materials to use in your next presentation.

Why Handouts Are Important

Used correctly, handouts can become a valuable ally in transferring a message from idea into action.

In the 1960s Marshall McCluhan said the medium is the message. In the 1990s I believe handouts support the message. They can make the difference between an average presentation and a great one. Yet, often handouts are overlooked. Used correctly, handouts can become a valuable ally in transferring a message from idea into action. As you are making a presentation, handouts will enable you to:

1. **Increase the listener's understanding and use of the information presented.**
   Have you ever been to a conference or workshop where people were frantically taking notes on everything the presenter said or everything they saw on a visual? As a matter of fact, the members of the audience were probably writing so much that they really didn't have much time to reflect on what the presenter was saying. They probably did not have time to think about any application or implication that the content may have had for them.

Handouts can help you avoid this situation in your presentations. By providing each participant with a handout, you enable listeners to focus more on the presentation and take fewer, more appropriate notes. What's more, the handout provides the listener with support materials so they can reflect on and integrate the content of the presentation after the session is over. Handouts insure that the audience takes away the key ideas of the presentation.

By providing each participant with a handout, you enable listeners to focus more on the presentation and take fewer, more appropriate notes.

2. **Engage the audience at a deeper level as they interact with the handout.**
   I believe writing crystallizes thought and thought produces action. If a handout allows space for writing and listeners take notes based on their thoughts and reactions to the material, they are more likely to put those ideas into action. My motto is: Don't just think it, ink it!

3. **Keep the audience's attention focused on the subject.**
   The average speaker speaks at a rate of about 120 to 180 words per minute. The audience thinks at a rate roughly 10 times faster. Interacting with a handout helps keep listeners' minds from wandering because of the gap between the rate the presenter is speaking and the rate that listeners are thinking.

4. **Present more information than can be covered in the presentation.**
   Handouts can help you expand the scope of what you can cover. Not only can you document the key points of your presentation, but you can also provide additional information listeners can digest after the session.

6

One format I've found effective is to divide my handout content into three areas—Need-to-know items, nice-to-know facts, and need-to-be-able-to-find materials. The need-to-know items I print on white paper. I will cover all of these pages in the presentation. The nice-to-know facts are supplementary. I print these on a different color paper and place them in an appendix. I may or may not make reference to this value-added material in the presentation. The need-to-be-able-to-find material I print on yellow paper. This is a reference section so if listeners need the information they can look it up in the "yellow pages."

5. **Create a positive impression before the presentation even begins.**
   A well-executed handout says to the audience that the presenter is prepared. A strong title, clean layout, inviting graphics, and plenty of white space for notes help set positive expectations for a good presentation.

6. **Insure that the presenter is prepared for the presentation.**
   Have you ever gone to a presentation where there was no handout and the presentation seemed off the cuff, disjointed, or not as organized as it could be? Preparing a handout forces the presenter to be more prepared than he or she otherwise would be. Developing the handout reinforces the presenter's understanding of the flow and content of the presentation. Just the very fact that the handout needs to be ready a day, a week, or a month before the presentation helps guarantee that the presenter has additional time to digest the content, even if it is on a subconscious level.

> **Preparing a handout forces the presenter to be more prepared than he or she otherwise would be.**

Almost anyone who has ever given the same presentation more than once realizes that the first presentation is not as good as the second. In the process of giving it the first time, you see things you could have done better or differently. Maybe you even discover an order or arrangement that works more effectively. Having to prepare a handout in advance helps to minimize that first presentation shakeout.

Some of the bugs are uncovered in the process of developing support materials. Preparation of this kind is invaluable to improving your delivery of the presentation.

7. **Help presenters, especially nonprofessional ones, get through the first few critical minutes of a presentation.**
   By having the audience look at the handout, you can use it as a track for the presentation and give the participants an overview of the major blocks of content you will cover. List your objectives at the front of the handout. This way, as you cover the objectives, the audience's focus is on the handout, not on you, and you may be a little more relaxed.

   > List your objectives at the front of the handout.

8. **Establish a presenter's authority, knowledge, and credibility.**
   An extensive, well-laid-out handout creates a polished, professional image. Putting an extensive biosketch in the front also can establish the presenter's authority. In every presentation that I do, the first page of my handout is a title page and the second is an extensive biosketch. The content of the biosketch is related to why I have the right to present on the subject. Then, even if I am not given an introduction or if the introduction isn't a very good one, the audience can get an idea of my authority by reading the biosketch. Also, some participants want more information about a presenter than is normally given in an introduction.

6

When to Hand Out a Handout

Distribute handouts at the beginning of a presentation.

Frequently I'm asked at what point during a presentation handouts should be distributed. For me, the best strategy always has been either before the presentation or very near the beginning.

I've heard presenters say, "Don't worry about taking notes. It's all in the handout you'll get at the end." As the presentation continues and I see various visuals, I find myself wondering (meanwhile, not listening to the presentation), "Will this be in the handout?" Not wanting to take a chance, I become more preoccupied with trying to copy all of the visuals than I am in relating the visual to the content being presented.

I've heard presenters argue that if they provide a handout at or near the beginning, people will simply read the handout and not listen to the presentation. I think this point is a design issue, not a timing one. If a handout is an exact copy of the text of a presentation, the audience's attention may wander, but by varying the look of the handout formats, you can keep the audience more tuned into the presentation, rather than less.

What to Put in a Handout

There are numerous materials you can include in a handout or resource manual that will enhance your presentation. Here is a rundown of the most effective items. Tailor your handout to your presentation by picking and choosing from these options.

◆ **A biographical sketch of the presenter**
   I often will place my biosketch as the second or third page of a handout. Why? Because even with a strong introduction (which most often is appropriate only for larger groups), the introduction may not say all there is to say about my ability to present on the subject. A written biosketch can provide more depth and later serve as a reference point as an audience member shares the presentation concepts with people who were not present.

A biosketch perhaps is even more important for in-company presentations. Just because you work for a company does not mean that you will have instant credibility with other employees. It also does not guarantee that they will be well-informed about who you are and what you've accomplished. The reverse may be true. You may have less face credibility than someone walking through the door from another firm.

◆ **Exact copies of visuals**
Many presentation and graphics packages can print monochrome copies of the visuals you will use in your presentation in one-, two-, four-, or even six-to-the-page formats. When the visuals incorporate strong graphics that convey and reinforce what the text is saying, they provide another way to anchor the key presentation points in the minds of listeners.

◆ **Partial visuals**
These are the same ones that the audience will see in the presentation, perhaps with even more detail. The main difference is you have replaced one or more of the key words in each visual with an underlined space. As the key words are mentioned in the presentation, the audience can complete the handout by filling in the blanks. As a matter of fact, there is almost a compulsion to do so. Listeners are curious about what goes in the spaces and don't like blanks left empty. This type of handout helps keep the audience focused on the point of the presentation at hand and often generates more writing than simply the key word. Remember: writing crystallizes thought and thought produces action.

Writing crystallizes thought and thought produces action.

6

◆ **A List of points or a checklist**
A list of the points you intend to cover in your presentation will help to keep the audience tuned in and will provide a convenient place for note taking. Also, checklists are always useful. If you are presenting a process, give your audience a checklist of the steps in the process. If a topic has several parts (for example, the nine basic parts of a brochure), a checklist that can be physically checked off will help the audience keep track of each part.

◆ **A glossary**
When you are using terms that your audience may not understand, by all means include a glossary as part of your handout. Listeners will appreciate having unfamiliar terms explained. Often people don't want to admit they don't know a term.

◆ **Lists**
People like lists—lists of additional resources, lists of books or articles that relate to the topic, lists of the 10 best or worst practices, etc.

◆ **Diagrams or flowcharts**
These are helpful whether they are explained in the presentation or not. For example, in a seminar I do on developing proposals, I use a flowchart showing the entire process of developing a training program. If I don't have time to explain it in a presentation, I'll make a brief reference to the flowchart, so that the audience is aware of it. The flowchart increases the overall value of the presentation because listeners realize that there is more in-depth information in the handout, including a complete diagram that they can use afterwards.

◆ **Article reprints**
These can be useful additions to the appendix or reference section of a handout.

◆ **Statistical data**
If a seminar includes any type of statistics, participants appreciate having the data in written form so they can refer to it later.

◆ **Discussion sheets**
In many presentations I ask the audience to interact in small groups. When this is the case, a discussion sheet with the questions I want the group to discuss or the directions I want them to follow helps accomplish the task with a minimum of confusion. This way the audience members don't have to remember exactly what they were supposed to do. It is written down for them.

◆ **Case studies**
Case studies can be valuable additions to both presentations and handouts. For example, in a presentation about change, you might introduce two case studies that illustrate resistance to change—one focusing on personal change and the other on business change. You can begin by referring the participants to the case studies in the handout and instruct them to discuss the cases in small groups. Then, follow up the discussion with a second project sheet. On this sheet the participants can note their reactions to the two cases and apply what they learned to their own situations.

6

◆ **Forms**
Everybody wants to save time and work. If you have a useful form that participants can reproduce and use, providing a sample copy will enhance both your handout and your presentation.

◆ **An action idea page**

In most presentations, the speaker wants the audience to act on ideas and information. Usually the ideas are scattered throughout the presentation and handout. I often provide a single page where audience members can record the ideas they most want to use. Several times during the presentation, I'll ask the audience to turn to the action idea page, reflect on the presentation, and jot down action ideas. If time permits, I'll have the listeners share their action ideas in small groups, and then have a few of the groups share one action idea that came out of their discussions. This procedure serves as a review of the presentation, reinforces the concepts (because the action ideas are developed by the audience, not by me), and helps to highlight key points that I want to stress.

◆ **Evaluation forms**

While conferences often have general evaluation forms, I frequently find it helpful to include my own evaluation form as the last page of a handout. Then, at the beginning of the presentation, I point out the evaluation form. I also ask the audience members to remove the forms and keep them handy so they can complete them whenever they choose. This way the audience knows at the beginning of the presentation which items I want them to critique.

A handout can alter how audience members perceive what they are getting from a presentation.

Handouts Can Make the Difference!

As you can see from this chapter, the handout is not just a frill or something "nice to do." It can significantly impact the effectiveness of a presentation as well as the value that the audience takes away from a program. A handout can alter how audience members perceive what they are getting from a presentation. Handouts can make a difference.

Self-Check: Chapter 6 Review

Indicate True or False for each of the statements below.
Suggested answers are given on page 91.

_____1. Handouts can provide more information than the
presentation can cover.

_____2. The credibility of the presenter can be enhanced
through an effective handout.

_____3. A partial copy of the visuals used in a presentation can
be part of the handout.

_____4. Handouts should be distributed after the presentation.

_____5. Giving the handout during the presentation only
distracts from the presenter.

6

Chapter *Seven*

Presentation Problems and Solutions

Chapter Objectives

▶ Understand several problems people encounter in presenting.

▶ Be able to select from a number of solutions to those problems.

In this book you have learned why high-impact presentations are important, the types of presentations you can give, and how to plan and execute an effective presentation. But even after reviewing all of this information, you still may have some problems with presentations that have not been addressed. To help you, I have outlined some additional suggestions for handling presentations.

Problem 1: My Presentation Is Boring

Is your presentation really boring? Or is it your handouts? or your visuals? Or is it your timing, pacing, and voice inflections? Here are some techniques to consider:

◆ **Try using fresh readable typestyles in your handout.**
Using two different typestyles can make your handout look more appealing. A serif typestyle will increase readability.

◆ **Use appropriate graphics to reinforce key points.**
Don't simply throw in some clip art, but choose graphics that fit the message you're conveying. Graphics should ALWAYS visually reinforce the content.

◆ **Make your visuals interesting by adding color and graphics.**
Unless your visuals are color photographs, though, limit yourself to two or three colors on a visual.

> Graphics should ALWAYS visually reinforce the content.

◆ **When it comes to delivering your presentation, consider practicing vocal emphasis.**
Rather than speaking in a flat monotone, deliberately emphasize key words. Here's an exercise to help you understand how to do this. Take this sentence and repeat it five times. Each time you say it aloud, emphasize the word in bold type.

I did not say he stole the money. (Who did?)
I did not **say** he stole the money. (How did I communicate it?)
I did not say **he** stole the money. (Who did I say stole it?)
I did not say he **stole** the money. (How did he get it?)
I did not say he stole the **money.** (What did he steal?)

This exercise shows how inflection or emphasis changes meaning—even if the words are the same. Take several key sentences from your presentation. Write them out. Repeat them aloud and each time change the emphasis. Which emphasis is the one you want to use to drive home your point?

7

◆ **Raise (or lower) the volume of your voice to emphasize key points.**
Changing the volume of a key word or phrase can enliven your presentation and insure your audience gets the point. Practice these sentences. Raise or lower your voice volume on the words in bold type.

A journey of a **thousand miles** begins with a single step.
A journey of a thousand miles begins with a **single step.**

◆ **Stretch a word or phrase.**
Who can forget Billy Crystal's "You look aaabbbsoluuuttely mahhhhvelous!"? Or Ed McMahon's "Heeeere's Johnny!"?

Problem 2: I Have Too Many Vocal Pauses

Vocal pauses fill in silences, which don't really need to be filled. Vocal pauses include *um, er, uh, ok,* and *you know.* Here are some techniques to reduce vocal pauses.

◆ **Tape-record your presentation several times.**
Each time listen to the presentation with a sheet of paper and note each vocal pause when it first occurs. Then, add a hash mark beside it each additional time it occurs. Being aware of when and where the vocal pauses come will help reduce the number of them in each subsequent taping.

◆ **Have someone observe your presentation, making note of the number and type of vocal pauses.**

◆ **Deliberately plan for some pauses in your presentation and then actually pause.**
Let the eloquence of silence work its magic for you!

Problem 3: I Get Nervous Before and During a Presentation

First, understand that there's nothing wrong with some nervousness. It's when you are not nervous at all that you are in trouble of being overconfident and perhaps too casual and sloppy. But if the thought of presenting brings absolute terror, then there's a problem. Here are some techniques and strategies to help reduce that nervousness to the point where it's an aid rather than an adversary:

◆ **Prepare, prepare, prepare**
Lack of preparation can be a significant cause of nervousness—and it should be. Doing your homework is a must for a high-impact presentation. If you've mastered the material, you can focus on delivery.

◆ **Practice, practice, practice**
Especially master your opening and closing. Practice them. Audiotape them. Even videotape them. Also, become familiar with your visuals and any equipment you will be using. Mastering them will enable you to focus on your audience. Practicing will reduce your nervousness.

Practicing will reduce your nervousness.

7

◆ **Breathe, breathe, breathe**
Before any presentation, I make sure I am alone for a few minutes and take some deep, slow breaths from my diaphragm. I also press my thumbs and forefingers together as I breathe to form a physical connection with the breathing. Anytime I feel nervousness rising during a presentation, I press my thumb and forefinger together. This helps me to recall my relaxed state before the presentation. It reminds me to take a slow, deep breath during the presentation.

◆ **Identify, identify, identify**
If you feel nervous about an upcoming presentation, take time to identify your specific fears and concerns. For example, if you're afraid you'll drop your notes and be disorganized, outline the worst possible case about the fear.

■ People will think I'm totally incompetent and have no knowledge of my subject. I'll be fired.

Then, counterattack.

■ Everybody is disorganized once in a while. Dropping my notes doesn't mean I'm incompetent. It means I dropped my notes. I don't know anyone that's been fired for dropping his or her notes.

Finally, problem solve.

■ I'll rehearse so I'm less note dependent. I'll number my notes so they're easy to reorganize. I'll put them in a binder.

That's All There Is to It

The techniques in this book will work for you. They have for thousands of others. They are all you need to reach even the most critical audiences.

Remember, a great presentation starts with a clearly defined purpose. Then, you must care enough to plan and prepare. Finally, you must add the passionate belief that you can use each presentation to make a difference. These are the secrets to being a high-impact presenter.

Remember, a great presentation starts with a clearly defined purpose.

7

Answers to Chapter Reviews

Chapter 1 Review (page 13)

1. True
2. True
3. False
4. True
5. True
6. False
7. True

Chapter 2 Review (page 35)

1. Solving a Problem
2. Providing Information
3. Selling a Product, Service, or Strategy
4. Obtaining a Decision
5. Teaching a Skill

Chapter 3 Review (page 46)

1. True
2. True
3. False
4. True
5. True
6. False

Chapter 4 Review (page 61)

1. True
2. True
3. False
4. False
5. True
6. True

Chapter 5 Review (page 73)

1. False
2. True
3. True
4. True
5. False
6. False
7. True

Chapter 6 Review (page 83)

1. True
2. True
3. True
4. False
5. False